MALALA

My story of standing up for girls' rights

MALALA YOUSAFZAI
with PATRICIA McCORMICK

Abridged and adapted by Sarah J. Robbins

Illustrations by Joanie Stone

wren

Published in Great Britain in 2018 by Wren & Rook
First published in the USA in 2018 by Little, Brown & Company

ISBN: 9781526361592
E-book ISBN: 9781526361585
10 9 8 7 6 5

Wren & Rook
An imprint of
Hachette Children's Group
Part of Hodder & Stoughton
Carmelite House
50 Victoria Embankment
London EC4Y 0DZ

An Hachette UK Company
www.hachette.co.uk
www.hachettechildrens.co.uk

Printed in the United Kingdom

To those children all over the world who have no access to education, to those teachers who bravely continue teaching, and to anyone who has fought for their basic human rights and education.

CONTENTS

Prologue

• • • •

I Am Malala

When I close my eyes, I can see my bedroom. The bed is unmade because I've rushed out for school, late for an exam. On my desk, my school schedule is open to the page dated 9 October 2012.

I can hear the neighbourhood kids playing in the alley behind our home. I can hear my little brothers fighting over the TV remote. I can smell rice cooking as my mother works in the kitchen. Then I hear my father's deep voice, calling out my nickname.

"***Jani*,**" he says, which is Persian for "dear one."

I left my beloved home in Pakistan that morning – planning to dive back into bed when I returned from school – and ended up a world away.

When I open my eyes, I am in my new bedroom. It is in a sturdy brick house in a damp and chilly place called Birmingham, England. Here, there is hardly a sound: no children laughing and yelling. No women downstairs chopping vegetables and gossiping with my mother. Through the thick walls between us, I hear someone in my family crying for home.

Then my father bursts through the front door, his voice booming. "*Jani!*" he says.

But there is worry in his voice, as if he fears I won't be there to reply. That is because it was not so long ago that somebody tried to hurt me – simply because

I was speaking out about my right to go to school.

• • • •

That day in October 2012 was an ordinary day. I was fifteen, in Year Ten, and I had overslept because I'd stayed up far too late the night before, studying for my exam.

My mother gently shook my shoulder. "Wake up, ***pisho***," she said, calling me *kitten* in ***Pashto***, the language spoken by my family's tribe, the Pashtun. "It's seven thirty, and you're late for school!"

I said a quick prayer to God. *If it is your will, **Allah**, may I please come in first on the exam? Oh, and thank you for all my success so far!*

I gulped down my breakfast while my youngest brother, Atal, whined. I was getting too much extra attention for speaking publicly about girls and boys having the same right to go to school, he complained.

"When Malala is prime minister some day, you can be her secretary," joked my father.

"No!" cried Atal, the little clown in the family. "She will be *my* secretary!"

I raced out the door and down the lane just in time to see the school bus crammed with other girls on their way to school.

I never saw my home again.

• • • •

That afternoon, my classmates and I stared down at our tests, trying to think over the honking horns and factory noises of our hometown of Mingora. By the end of the day, I was tired but happy. I knew I had done well.

I asked my best friend, Moniba, to wait with me for the late bus, so we could talk longer.

We told jokes and laughed until we stepped into the ***dyna***, the open-backed white truck that was our Khushal

School "bus".

As usual, our bus driver, Usman Bhai Jan, had a magic trick to show us. That day, he made a pebble disappear. No matter how hard we tried, we couldn't figure out his secret.

Nineteen girls, two teachers, and I bounced along Haji Baba Road: a mix of brightly coloured rickshaws, women in flowing robes, men on scooters, honking and zigzagging through the traffic. Our bus had no windows – just a yellowed plastic sheet that flapped against the side.

We were not more than three minutes from my house when the truck stopped suddenly. It was oddly quiet outside.

"It's so calm today," I said to Moniba. "Where are all the people?"

I don't remember anything after that.

Here's the story that's been told to me:

Two young men in white robes stepped in front of our truck. One of them jumped onto the back and leaned under the plastic sheet.

"Who is Malala?" he asked.

No one said a word, but a few girls looked in my direction. The man raised his arm and pointed at me. Some of the girls screamed, and I squeezed Moniba's hand.

Who is Malala? I am Malala, and this is my story.

PART ONE

• • • •

Before the Danger

1

As Free as a Bird

I am Malala Yousafzai, a girl like any other – although I do have my special talents.

I can crack the knuckles of my fingers and my toes whenever I want. I can beat someone twice my age at arm wrestling.

I like cupcakes but not sweets. And I don't think dark chocolate should be called chocolate at all.

I don't care for make-up and jewellery,

and I'm not a girly girl. But my favourite colour is pink.

I say that if you check a boy's rucksack, it will always be a mess. If you check his uniform, it will be dirty. This is not my opinion. This is just a fact.

I am a Pashtun, a member of a proud tribe of people spread across Afghanistan and Pakistan. My father, Ziauddin, and my mother, Toor Pekai, are from mountain villages. After they married, they moved to Mingora, the largest city in the Swat Valley, which is in the northwest of my beloved country Pakistan.

I was born in 1997 in the Swat Valley, which is known for its beauty: its tall mountains, green hills, and crystal clear rivers.

I am named for a brave young Pashtun girl named Malalai of Maiwind in Afghanistan. In a battle hundreds of years ago, Malalai inspired warriors with her courage. But I don't believe in fighting.

I say that even though I argue with my brother Khushal all the time. He is two years younger than me. We argue over who's the better student. Over who ate the last of the Wotsits. Over whatever you can think of.

My other brother, Atal, annoys me less. He is six years younger than me. He is quite good at chasing down the cricket ball when we kick it out-of-bounds. But he also makes up his own rules sometimes.

When I was younger, and these brothers came along, I had a little talk with God. *God*, I said, *you did not check with me before sending these two. They are quite inconvenient sometimes.*

Still, at home in Pakistan, my brothers and I ran like a pack of rabbits, playing tag, or hopscotch, or thief and police. Sometimes we rang the bell at someone else's house, then ran away and hid. Our favourite, though, was cricket, which we played day and night in the alley by our house or up on our flat roof.

When I'd had enough of my brothers,

I'd go downstairs and knock on the wall between our house and my friend Safina's. Two taps, that was our code. She'd tap in reply.

Safina is a couple of years younger than me, but we were very close. We often copied each other, but once, I thought she had gone too far, when my only toy – a pink plastic mobile phone my father had given me – went missing.

That afternoon, when I went to play with Safina, she had the same phone! She said it was hers, but I didn't believe her. When she wasn't looking, I took a pair of her earrings. The next day, a necklace.

When my mother found out, she was so upset she wouldn't look at me.

"Safina stole from me first!" I cried.

But that didn't matter to my mother: "You are older, Malala," she said. "You should have set a good example."

I felt shame, knowing that my father would be so disappointed in me.

But when he came home, he didn't scold me. He knew I was being hard on myself already. Instead, he told me that all children make mistakes – even heroes like Martin Luther King Jr., the American civil rights activist, and Mahatma Gandhi, the great peace activist of India.

Then he shared a saying that his father used to tell him: "A child is a child when he's a child, even if he's a prophet." He meant that even people who go on to do great things can do childish things, because they were children once.

Our Pashtun tribe believes in ***badal***, or revenge – one bad action must be answered by another. I thought Safina had stolen from me, so I stole from her. But my taste of badal was bitter. Safina and I quickly got back to being friends, and I vowed then that I would never seek revenge again.

• • • •

For as long as I can remember, our house had been full of people: a never-ending stream of neighbours, relatives, and friends of my father. One of the most important parts of being a Pashtun is always opening your door to a visitor.

In the back of our house, my mother and the women would gather to cook and laugh and talk about new clothes, jewellery, and other ladies in the neighbourhood. My father and the men would sit in the men's guest room and drink tea and talk politics.

I would sometimes wander away from the children's games, tiptoe through the crowd of women, and join the men, drinking in every word about the big world beyond our valley.

After a while I would go to the women, to listen to their whispers and their laughter. My favourite part: the scarves and veils covering their heads were gone. Their long dark hair and pretty faces – made up with lipstick and henna – were lovely to see.

Where I grew up, women follow the code of **purdah**, where they are separated from men and cover themselves in public. Some, like my mother, draped scarves over their faces. Others covered themselves with long, flowing black robes, and sometimes even black gloves and socks. They hid every bit of skin – even their eyes.

But when the women were away from men, they would show their beautiful faces – and I would see a whole new world. I always wondered how it felt to live in hiding.

Even as a little girl, I told my parents that no matter what other girls did, *I* would never cover my face like that. My mother and some of our other relatives were shocked. But my father said I could do as I wished.

"Malala will live as free as a bird," he told everyone.

I knew that I was the apple of my father's

eye. A rare thing for a Pakistani girl.

When a boy is born in Pakistan, it's cause for celebration. Gifts are placed in the baby's cot. The boy's name is inscribed on the family tree. But when a girl is born, no one visits the parents.

My father paid no mind to these customs. I've seen my name – in bright blue ink – right there among the male names of our family tree. Mine was the first female name in three hundred years.

Sometimes, when I thought about the future, I remembered the kite-flying contests we had as kids. The boys who wanted to win tried to cut the other kids' kite strings. I always felt a bit sad to see the pretty kites sputter to the ground.

I worried that my future could be cut down just like those kites – simply because I was a girl. As Safina and I got older, we'd be expected to cook and clean for our brothers. We couldn't be lawyers or engineers, fashion designers or artists – or most other things we dreamed of. And we wouldn't be allowed to go outside our homes without a male relative to accompany us.

I often wondered how free I could ever really be.

My father was hopeful.

"Look at this girl," said my father with pride when I learned to read. "She is destined for the skies!"

I was far luckier than most girls in one other way, too: my father ran a school, the Khushal School. It was a humble place with nothing more than blackboards and chalk – and it was right next to a smelly river. But to me, it was a paradise.

My father did every job in the school. He was the teacher, the principal, and the janitor. After he paid the school's bills, not much money was left for food. But the school had been my father's dream, and we were all happy to be living it.

My parents tell me that when I was first learning to walk, I toddled into the empty classrooms and gave lessons in my own baby talk. As I grew, I sat in on classes. I couldn't wait to wear the uniforms I saw the big girls wearing when they arrived each day: *shalwar kamiz* – a long deep blue shirt and loose white trousers – and a white headscarf. When it was finally time for me to be a student, I was so excited I could hardly contain myself.

You could say I grew up in a school. The school was my world, and my world was the school.

2

A Magic Pencil

Every spring and autumn, my family visited one of my favourite places on earth: Shangla, the mountain village where my parents grew up. It was a four-hour trip by bus, along roads that followed the Swat River on one side and hugged sheer cliffs on the other. As we climbed higher and higher, my brothers pointed out the cars or buses that had fallen into the valley below. Eventually the air turned cool and crisp, and we saw nothing but mountain after mountain. Mountain, mountain, mountain, and just a sliver of sky.

Though most people in the village were very poor, our family always put on a feast when we arrived. Especially when it was the holiday of Small Eid, which marks the end of **Ramadan** – the holiest month of the year in our religion, Islam. During Ramadan, followers of Islam, who are called Muslims, go without food all day, from sunrise to sunset, to focus on prayer and to remember all that God has given us. On Small Eid, our family shared bowls of chicken and rice, spinach and lamb, apples, pretty yellow cakes, and kettles of sweet milky tea. We brought boxes of sweets and other gifts we had stacked on top of the bus.

What Is Ramadan? What Is Small Eid? What Is Big Eid?

• • • • •

Ramadan is the ninth month of the Islamic calendar. It is considered the holiest month, in which Muslims all over the world reflect on their faith by praying with increased devotion, reading the **Holy Quran**, spending time with family, giving to charity, and fasting each day from sunrise to sunset. (Families and friends often share a meal together after the sun goes down.)

"Small Eid," which is also known as Eid al-Fitr, is a three-day celebration marking the end of Ramadan, with feasts, family visits, and gifts – especially for kids.

In Dhu al-Hijjah, which is the twelfth month of the Islamic calendar, is the Eid ul-Azha, or "the feast of sacrifice." This is Big Eid, and it is celebrated to commemorate the sacrifice of the prophet Abraham in the way of Allah. The spirit of Eid ul-Azha lies in the concept of sharing Allah's blessing with your loved ones as well as the underprivileged people around you.

In my cousins' eyes, I was a city girl. They teased me because I didn't like to go barefoot and wore clothes from the market, not homemade like theirs. If only they knew that people from real cities like Islamabad, the capital of Pakistan, would have thought that *I* was a country girl.

When we were together in the village, we all lived the country life: when the rooster crowed, we spilled out of the houses to greet the day. We ate honey from the hive, and green plums sprinkled with salt. None of us had toys or books, so we played hopscotch and cricket in a gully.

Life for women in the mountains was not easy. There were no proper shops, no hospitals or female doctors. Like women in Mingora, the women of Shangla also covered their faces. They could not meet or speak to men who were not their close relatives. None of them could read – not even my own mother, who'd grown up in the village.

Many girls in the village didn't go to school.

People thought it was less important than it was for boys, since a girl would be married off at a young age to live with her husband's family. "Why send her to school?" the men often say. "She doesn't need an education to run a house."

I would never talk back to my elders. In my culture, one must never disrespect one's elders – even if they are wrong. But when I saw how hard these women's lives were, I was confused and sad.

Why were women treated so poorly in our country? I asked my father.

He told me that life was even worse for women in Afghanistan, the country next to ours, where a dangerous group called the **Taliban** had taken over. The Taliban disapproved of most actions seen as Western – something that might be acceptable in the United States, Canada, or European countries. They claimed that Western beliefs and behaviours were not appropriate based on their very strict version of Islam, one that twists the true Islamic beliefs in a way that threatens the rights of others.

In Afghanistan, schools for girls had been destroyed, and all women were forced to wear a head-to-toe veil that had only a tiny window for their eyes. It was called a **burqa**. Women were banned from laughing out loud or wearing nail polish, and they were sometimes put in prison for walking without a male family member.

Hearing such things, I thanked God that I lived in Pakistan, where a girl was free to go to school. I didn't realise that the Taliban weren't only in Afghanistan. There was another group in Pakistan, and they would soon come to cast a dark shadow over my sunny childhood.

My father told me not to worry. "I will protect your freedom, Malala," he said. "Carry on with your dreams."

• • • •

By the time I was eight years old, my father's school had expanded to three buildings and had more than eight hundred students. Because most families paid to send their children to school, our family finally had enough money to buy a TV! Sometimes Safina and I watched *Shaka Laka Boom Boom*, a show about a boy named Sanju, who could make anything real by drawing it with a magic pencil. If he was hungry, he drew a bowl of curry, and it appeared. If he was in danger, he drew a policeman. He was a little hero, always protecting people.

I began to dream about a magic pencil of my own. At night I would pray, *God, please give me Sanju's pencil. I won't tell anyone. Just leave it in my cupboard. I will use it to make everyone happy.* Then I would check the drawer. But the pencil was never there.

I really wanted the magic pencil when my mother asked me to take rubbish to the dump near our house. Then I could have erased it all: the smell, the rats, the giant mountain of rotting food. I was about to toss our potato peels and eggshells onto the rubbish heap one afternoon when I saw something move. I jumped.

It was a girl my age. She and some boys nearby were sorting through rubbish. I wanted to talk to them, but I was scared.

Later that night I asked my father about the children. Why weren't they in school?

He told me that these children sold what they found at the dump to help feed their

families; if they went to school, their families would go hungry.

I realised then that God must have been showing me what my life might be like if I couldn't go to school. There was no such thing as a magic pencil to change the world: *I* would have to do something. But what?

I wrote a letter to God, asking for *the strength and courage to make the world a better place.* I signed my letter, rolled it up, tied it to a piece of wood, placed a dandelion on top, and floated it in a stream that flows into the Swat River. Surely God would find it there.

As much as I wanted to help the children from the dump, my mother wanted to help everyone. She often had an extra pot of rice and chicken to feed a poor family in our neighbourhood.

I asked her once why she always gave food away. "We have known what it is like to be hungry, pisho," she said. "We must never forget to share what we have."

3

• • • •

Warnings

One night I opened our door to six elders from our village as well as a frowning man who said he was a **mufti**, or an Islamic scholar. My father shooed me into the other room, but I heard every word.

The man said he had a problem with our school. "I am representing good Muslims, and we all think you should close your girls' high school," he said. "Teenage girls should not be going to school. They should be in purdah."

This mufti clearly believed that girls did not have equal rights to an education. What we knew, but the mufti did not, was that his own niece attended my father's school in secret.

As my father debated with the mufti, one of the other men spoke up. He was surprised to see multiple copies of the Holy Quran, our holy book, in our home.

"Of course!" my father said. "I am a Muslim."

My father and the men came to a compromise: older girls would enter through a different gate.

Even as the door shut behind them, I had a knot in my stomach, thinking of the mufti. I knew this man was mistaken. There was nothing un-Islamic about girls going to school.

My parents sent me to an open-air **madrasa**, a school where boys and girls together studied the Holy Quran, which we believe to be the word of God, or Allah. The Holy Quran is written in Arabic. I loved the sounds of the prayers and the stories about how to live a life according to the teachings of the sacred book.

While my madrasa classmates could recite the Holy Quran, they didn't learn what the words actually meant. I was the only one who wanted to learn the meanings of the Arabic words and who did the rest of my lessons – science, maths, and literature – at the Khushal School.

I didn't think much of this difference until later, after the mufti's visit to our house. One day the neighbourhood children were choosing up sides for a game of cricket, and one of the boys said he didn't want me on his team.

"Our school is better than yours," he said, as if that explained things. He meant the madrasa.

I didn't agree one bit. "My school is the better one," I said.

"Your school is bad," he insisted. "It is not

on the straight path of Islam."

I didn't know how to respond, but I knew he was wrong. The Khushal School was the best place. In a country where women aren't allowed in public without a man, the other girls and I could travel far and wide inside the pages of our books. In a country where we would soon be expected to keep away from our male schoolmates, we ran as free as the wind.

We didn't know where our education would take us. We just wanted a chance to learn in peace. Once we dropped our schoolbags inside the Khushal School, we had the same worries as any schoolkid: who would get the highest mark on the day's test, and who would sit with whom at break? We worked hard and we laughed together.

How could a place where I learned so much and laughed so much be bad?

PART TWO

• • • •

A Shadow Over Our Valley

4

Radio Mullah

We were visiting relatives who lived nearby one evening when I heard a strange sobbing on the radio. At first, it sounded like just another **imam**, or religious leader, giving advice. Pray daily, he said. The women murmured in approval.

Then he began to cry. *Stop listening to music*, he begged. *Stop going to movies. Stop dancing. Stop*, he begged, *or God will send another earthquake to punish us all.* Some of the women began to cry, memories of the previous year's earthquake – one of the worst ever to hit our region – fresh in their minds.

I wanted to tell them that it wasn't true: an earthquake is explained by science. But the women had no education and were raised to believe their religious leaders. So they were frightened.

My father told us not to listen to this man, whom people called the Radio **Mullah**, which is another word for imam. But my friends at school began to repeat what he said almost word for word. All music was **haram**, said the mullah, which meant that it was forbidden by Islam. Only his radio station was permitted. Men should grow their hair and beards long, he said, and women should stay at home in purdah quarters at all times: they should go out only in emergencies and only wearing a burqa and only with a male relative.

Many people admired how the mullah talked about the importance of daily prayer.

They didn't have faith in our government, which they felt had not helped enough after the earthquake, so they agreed with his idea of bringing back Islamic law.

The voice on the radio belonged to Fazlullah, one of the leaders of the group that had helped many people after the earthquake. Now he was using that disaster to make them feel afraid.

• • • •

At home, I began serving tea to my father and the other men so I could continue sitting in on their discussions without being noticed.

In those days there were only two topics of conversation: the Radio Mullah and the fighting just across the border in Afghanistan. For the past several years, the United States and others had been fighting a war to defeat the Taliban government in Afghanistan, which was protecting **al-Qaeda**, another dangerous group with similar beliefs.

The *Taliban*. As soon as I would hear that word, I'd think back to the conversation I'd had with my father when we were in Shangla. The Taliban seemed like something far away then, something bad in a distant place. Fazlullah was connected to the Taliban in Pakistan, and my father warned the other men there would come a day when the Taliban would reach our valley.

For the first time, it occurred to me that our world was changing before my eyes, and not for the better.

• • • •

The Radio Mullah cast a dark cloud of fear over our valley.

I arrived at school one day to find my friends all huddled in the corner, talking about the radio show the night before. Fazlullah had announced that schools for girls were haram – forbidden by the Holy Quran.

Then in July 2007, he called for people to rise up in violence against the government.

My father said our family should do its best to ignore the mullah's talk. "We must live a full life, if only in our hearts," he said.

And so, as usual, our dinner conversations were about things of the mind: Einstein and Newton, poets and philosophers. And, as usual, my brothers and I fought over the remote, over who got the best marks, over anything and everything.

Then Fazlullah joined forces with another Taliban group and announced that women could not go out in public at all. Suddenly, everywhere I looked, the Taliban seemed to sprout like weeds.

There were rumours that the Radio Mullah's men were listening at doors. If they heard someone watching TV, which they called a sin, they would bash the door in and then smash the TV to bits.

My brothers and I didn't understand how wrestlers with funny names and a little boy with a magic pencil were so bad. But every time there was a knock on the door, we jumped.

Eventually we moved our TV to a cupboard. Then if strangers came to the door, they wouldn't see it.

How had the mullah got so much power? And why was no one prepared to defy him?

• • • •

When Fazlullah started announcing the names of schoolgirls on his radio show, my mother insisted that I never walk to school by myself. She was afraid that I would be seen alone in my school uniform by the Taliban.

The Khushal School had fallen under the shadow of the Radio Mullah. Every day, I noticed that a few more of our classmates had stayed at home. One of our teachers told my father that he would no longer teach girls.

I shuddered to hear the stories of Fazlullah's men punishing the men and women who disobeyed him. What was becoming of my city? What would become of us?

God, I said when I went to bed, *please protect my city and its people.*

• • • •

My father went to a meeting to speak out against the Taliban. And after that, he traveled to Islamabad to urge the government to protect its citizens. While he was away, I took on the nightly job of going around the house once, twice, often three times, making sure all the doors and windows were locked.

Sometimes my father came home quite late. Sometimes he would sleep at a friend's house in case he was being followed. He was protecting us by staying away, but he could not protect us from worrying. Those nights, I heard my mother praying until all hours.

My father was a simple school headmaster, but he was like a falcon, daring to fly where others would not go. My mother was the one with her feet firmly planted on the ground.

• • • •

One day we found a letter for my father taped to the school gate.

Sir, it read, *the school you are running is Western and infidel. You teach girls and you have a uniform that is un-Islamic. Stop this or you will be in trouble and your children will weep and cry for you.*

It was signed ***Fedayeen*** *of Islam* – devotees of Islam.

The Taliban had threatened my father. Now I was afraid.

The next day, my father replied to the Taliban in a letter to the newspaper. *Please don't harm my schoolchildren*, he wrote, *because the God you believe in is the same God they pray to every day.*

Our phone started ringing that night: friends calling to thank my father for the letter.

My father had always been a busy man. But

now, each time he left home, I wondered: will he come back?

My father decided that our school uniforms would change: boys would no longer wear the "Western" uniform of shirt and trousers; they would switch to the traditional tunic and pants of the shalwar kamiz. I still wore my blue-and-white shalwar kamiz, but the Taliban said girls should not wear the white shalwar because then they would look like boys. The uniform I once loved now made me feel like a criminal.

What Is Shalwar Kamiz?

• • • •

The shalwar kamiz is a traditional outfit worn by men and women of all ages. It refers to a pair of long, baggy trousers (the shalwar), which is often paired with a long tunic (the kamiz). Specific styles differ by region, but they are all usually made of light material and are quite comfortable!

Then I thought: *what have I done wrong that I should be afraid? All I want to do is go to school. And that is not a crime. That is my right.* Besides, I was the daughter of Ziauddin Yousafzai, the man who had dared to talk back to the Taliban. I would hold my head high – even if my heart was quaking.

Sometimes, when I was feeling afraid, a tiny voice in my heart whispered to me: "why don't *you* fight to make Pakistan a better place?"

Due to the attention my father was getting, I had been approached by journalists who wanted to hear from a girl about being forbidden from school. I had recently done interviews about girls' education with national TV news channels, and although I had been nervous, I had made it through. And I had liked it.

So I told myself, "I will continue this fight for peace and democracy in my country."

I was only ten, but I knew then that somehow I would find a way.

5

What Terrorism Feels Like

I was at school one day when we heard a fearsome roaring from outside. Everyone – students and teachers – ran out to the courtyard and looked up. A swarm of black army helicopters darkened the sky. They whipped the wind around us, stirred up a storm of dirt and sand, and drowned out our voices with their roar.

Something landed on the ground at our feet. *Plunk! Plunk! Plunk!* We screamed – then we cheered. Toffees! Soldiers were tossing sweets down to us. We laughed as we caught toffees. Sweets were falling from the sky! And peace was on its way!

We'd been praying for someone to stand up to Fazlullah and his men with their black turbans and big guns. Now our town was swarming with soldiers in green uniforms.

Fazlullah's men disappeared practically overnight, like snow melting into the ground. But we knew they had not gone far, so Mingora remained a tense and frightened city. Each day after school my brothers and I would race home and lock the doors. No more playing cricket in the alley. No more hide-and-seek in the street. No more sweets from the sky.

• • • •

One evening we heard an announcement that we didn't understand. I knocked on the wall to Safina's house so someone could come to our house and explain the word *curfew*. Safina and her mother and brother told us it meant we had to stay indoors for certain hours of the day and always at night.

Later that night, bright white light flashed across the sky and lit up our rooms. Then: *boom!* A thud shook the ground. My brothers and I ran to our parents, and we all huddled together, shaking as we listened to the bombs drop. Each time we heard a noise, we gripped one another harder until we drifted off to sleep.

We hoped that the sound meant the army had defeated the Taliban. My father went to find out what had happened and returned with a frown. Our hearts sank when he told us what he had learned: the Taliban were going to take control of our valley.

The fighting between the army and the Taliban raged on for a year and a half. My brothers crowded my parents' bed, so I had to sleep on a pile of blankets on the floor. (Even in the middle of a war, I hated that my brothers stole my spot!) Strange as it sounds, we got used to the bombings.

I often spoke to God from my spot on the floor in my parents' room. *Bless us and protect us*, I said. I wished for peace for everyone. And, especially, peace for Swat. I tried to plug my ears and picture my prayers floating up to God.

Somehow we awoke each morning safe and sound. Then, one day, my prayer was answered. The army hadn't won, but it had at least driven the Taliban into hiding, if not away.

• • • •

Our school's doors were not always open during the fighting, but when they were, I was there. Once my friends and I moved to the upper school, our friendly competition got even more competitive. We didn't just want to get good marks; we wanted to get top marks.

Though we did each want to be the best, what mattered to us most was a teacher's appreciation. Seeing that helped us to think, *I* am *something!* For in a country where so many people consider it a waste to send girls to school, a teacher is the one who helps you believe in your dreams. Our upper-school headmistress, Madam Maryam, was bright and independent – everything I wanted to be. She had been to college. She had a job earning her own wage.

We had our school subjects, like algebra, chemistry and physics, but mostly what we talked about those days was the army and the Taliban. The people of Swat were caught in the middle. One friend used to like to annoy me by saying, "Taliban is good, army not good." And I always told her that when you are caught between two sides fighting, there is no good.

• • • •

Travelling to and from school had become frightening, so when I was safe at home, I just wanted to relax. One day I arrived ahead of my brothers and turned on the TV, but all I got was static. I tried every station. Nothing but static.

At first, I thought it was a power outage – we'd been having those a lot, but that night we found out that Fazlullah's men had switched off all the cable channels. With nothing to watch but the government television channel, we were all but cut off from the outside world.

Another day I found my father with his head in his hands. "Oh, jani," he said, "the world has gone mad." He told me that Fazlullah's men had destroyed a girls' school in a nearby town.

I felt my heart drop. I could not imagine why anyone would want to rob children of the chance to learn to read and write. Why was a school building such a threat to the Taliban?

Please, God, I prayed, *help us to protect our valley and to stop this violence.*

Every day, Fazlullah's men struck a new target. Stores, roads, bridges. And schools.

Most of the attacks were outside Mingora, but soon they got closer. One day I was cleaning dishes in the kitchen, and a bomb went off so close that the whole house rattled and the fan over the window fell.

I had grown up hearing the word *terrorism*, but only now did I understand it. Terrorism is different from war – where soldiers face one another in battle. Terrorism is going to sleep at night and not knowing what horrors the next day will bring. It is walking down your own street and not knowing whom you can trust. It is the enemy everywhere and the attacks coming out of nowhere.

Our family fell into a routine every time we heard a blast. We called to one another to make sure everyone was safe. Then we listened for the sirens. Then we prayed.

Still, this kind of random terror made us do strange things. My father started taking a different route home each evening in case someone was studying his routine. My mother avoided the market, and my brothers stayed inside on even the sunniest days. And since I had been in the kitchen both times blasts were near our house, I stayed as far from that room as possible. But how can a person live when she is afraid of a room in her own home?

Night-time was the worst.

Fazlullah's men carried out most of their attacks at night – especially the destruction of schools. In 2008 alone, the Taliban attacked two hundred schools. Every morning, before I rounded the corner on the way to the Khushal School, I closed my eyes and said a prayer – afraid to open them in case the school had been reduced to rubble overnight. This was what terrorism felt like.

One night, when a blast hit especially close to our home, I went to my father's side. "Are you scared now?" I asked.

"At night our fear is strong, jani," he said. "But in the morning, in the light, we find our courage again."

PART THREE

• • • •

Finding My Voice

6

A Chance to Speak

My father spoke out against the school bombings even though it was dangerous to do so. He also travelled to the capital to plead with the government for help.

My father was brave. My mother was worried. She would hug us close and pray over us before we left for school. She sat late into the night with her phone in her hand – trying not to call my father every hour.

At school, we wrote speeches about how we

felt about the Taliban's campaign to destroy girls' schools and about how much our own school meant to us. We planned to give our speeches during an assembly, and that day, a Pashto TV crew arrived at our school.

We were excited and surprised – we didn't think anyone cared what a group of girls had to say. I was a bit more comfortable in front of a camera than most girls. But even I was nervous.

We were a democracy at the Khushal School, so every girl would get a chance to speak. Girls talked about friends who had quit school out of fear and about how much we loved to learn.

Then Moniba, our public-speaking champion (and, of course, my best friend), spoke like a poet. "Because of the Taliban, the whole world is claiming we are terrorists," she said. "This is not the case. We Pashtuns are peace-loving. Our mountains, our trees, our flowers – everything in our valley is about peace."

I was speaking next, and as soon as they

put a microphone in front of me, the words came out sure and steady, strong and proud. Microphones made me feel as if I were speaking to the whole world.

"This is not the Stone Age," I said. "But it feels like we are going backward. Girls are getting more deprived of our rights." I spoke about how much I loved school and how important it was to keep learning. "We are afraid of no one, and we will continue our education. This is our dream."

I knew in that instant that it wasn't me, Malala, speaking; my voice was the voice of so many others who wanted to speak but couldn't. I was speaking with local journalists, but, still, I felt as if the wind would carry my words, the same way it scatters flower pollen in the spring, planting seeds all over the earth.

After that, I started a funny habit: looking in the mirror and giving speeches. I wouldn't see myself in the mirror; I would see hundreds of people listening to me.

I felt quite silly sometimes when I realised I was giving a speech to a mirror. Maybe I was still that little Malala who lectured to an empty classroom. But maybe it was something more.

Maybe that girl in the mirror, that girl who imagined speaking to the world, was the Malala I would become.

Throughout 2008, as our Swat was being attacked, I didn't stay silent. I spoke to local and national TV channels, radio, and newspapers – I spoke out to anyone who would listen.

7

A Schoolgirl's Diary

"After the fifteenth of January, no girl, whether big or little, shall go to school. Otherwise, you know what we can do. And the parents and the school head teacher will be responsible."

That was the news that came over Radio Mullah in late December 2008. I did not believe it at first. How could one man stop more than fifty thousand girls from going to school?

Some of my classmates tried to convince me of the danger. "The Taliban have already blown up hundreds of schools, and no one has done anything," said one.

We could be the ones to stop them, I argued. But within days we went from twenty-seven girls in our year to ten.

It was hard not to feel as if the families of those girls were simply surrendering to Fazlullah. I felt sad and frustrated, but I also understood. The fathers and brothers and uncles who made my friends stay home were doing so out of concern for their safety. Whenever I felt defeated, I'd have one of my talks with God. *Help us appreciate the school days that are left to us, God, and give us the courage to fight even harder for more.*

• • • •

I wondered what I would do if I couldn't go to school. Spend the rest of my life indoors, out of sight, with no TV to watch and no books to read? How would I complete my studies and become a doctor, which was my greatest hope at the time?

We tried to enjoy the days until 15 January, but every morning, someone arrived at school with another terrible story about Fazlullah's men attacking people who didn't live exactly the way the Taliban did. And now, we would be forbidden from going to school.

One afternoon I heard my father on the phone. "All the teachers have refused," he said. "They are too afraid. But I will see what I can do." He hung up and rushed out of the house.

I learned that he had been asked by a friend who worked at the BBC, the powerful British Broadcasting Corporation network, to find a female teacher or older student from the school to write a diary about life under the Taliban. The teachers said no. An older girl had agreed, but her father said it was too risky.

My father knew the Taliban were cruel, but even *they* wouldn't hurt a child, he wanted to say. But he respected the girl's father's decision and prepared to call the BBC with the bad news.

I was only eleven, and I knew he wanted someone older, but I said, "Why not me?"

I looked at my father's hopeful – nervous – face. I knew the diary might be read by people outside Pakistan. It was the BBC, after all.

My father had always stood by me. Could I stand by him? I knew that I could. I would do anything to be able to continue going to school. But first we went to my mother. If I didn't have her support, I wouldn't do it.

My mother gave us her answer with a verse from the Holy Quran. "Falsehood has to die," she said. "And truth has to come forward." God would protect me, she said, because my mission was a good one.

Our family didn't look at life and see danger. We saw possibility. We believed in hope. "Speaking up is the only way things will get better," my mother said.

I didn't know how to write a diary, so the BBC reporter helped me. Worried about my safety, he suggested that I use a fake name, so the Taliban wouldn't know who was writing the diary. He chose the name Gul Makai, which means "cornflower" and is the name of a heroine in a Pashtun folktale.

My first diary entry appeared on 3 January 2009, about two weeks before Fazlullah's deadline. The title was "I Am Afraid." I wrote about how hard it was to study or to sleep at night with the constant sounds of fighting in the hills outside town. And I described how I walked to school each morning, looking over my shoulder for fear I'd see a **Talib** following me.

The story of what was happening in Swat was there on the Internet for the whole world to see. It was as if God had at long last granted my wish for that magic pencil.

• • • •

My next diary entry was about how school was the centre of my life and about how proud I was to walk the streets of Mingora in my school uniform. For the next one, the BBC reporter asked me to write about some of the fighting in our area. That was news to him, but to me, what you experience every day is no longer news.

Sometimes I felt that I had no fear. Then, one day, on my way home from school, I heard a man's footsteps behind me. My heart stopped, but somehow my feet kept going, faster and faster, until I was far ahead of him. I ran home, shut the door, and, after a few seconds, peeked out at him. There he was, unaware of me, shouting at someone on his phone.

I laughed a bit at myself. "Malala," I thought, "there are real things to be afraid of. You don't need to imagine danger where there is none."

The real worry, it seemed to me, was being found out. And, of course, it was Moniba who first guessed the identity of Gul Makai. "I read a diary in the newspaper," she said one day at break. "The story sounds like our story, what happens in our school. It's you, isn't it?" she asked.

I had to tell Moniba the truth. But that made her even more angry. "How can you say you're my best friend when you're keeping such an important secret from me?" She turned around and left. And still I knew that she wouldn't tell anyone it was me.

My father revealed our secret. By accident. He told a reporter how scary it was for children just to walk to and from school. His own daughter, he said, thought a man on his phone was coming to hurt her. Just about everyone recognised this from the diary, and by April, my days as Gul Makai, secret diarist, would be over.

But the diary had done its job. Now a number of reporters were following the story of Fazlullah's attempt to shut down the girls' schools of Pakistan, including a man from a big newspaper in America, the *New York Times*.

8

• • • •

Class Dismissed?

A couple of days before the official school closing, my father took me to a meeting with two video journalists from the *New York Times*. They had wanted to follow him on the last day of school.

At the end of the meeting, one of them turned to me and asked, "What would you do if there comes a day when you can't go back to your valley and school?"

"That will not happen," I said, stubborn

and full of hope.

When he insisted that it might, I started to cry. I think that was when they decided to film me as well. On my last day of school, a two-man camera crew arrived to follow me from start to finish. I heard my father try to talk them out of this idea – he had given permission to film at school, not at home – but eventually he gave in, and the filming began.

"They cannot stop me. I will get my education," I told the cameraman. "This is our request to the world – save our schools, save our Pakistan, save our Swat." I didn't know that my words would reach many ears. Some in distant parts of the world. Some right in Swat, where the Taliban might hear.

Later that day, as my friends and I passed through the school gate and the video camera recorded our every move, it felt as if we were going to a funeral. Our dreams were dying.

Since we had all vowed to go to school on the last day, I was sad to see that most of

my classmates were absent. Then one more girl burst through the doors. Her father and brothers had forbidden her from going to school, but as soon as they left for the day, she sneaked out. What a strange world it was when a girl who wanted to go to school had to defy militants with machine guns – as well as her own family.

The teachers tried to act as if everything were normal. Some even gave us homework as if they'd see us again after the winter holiday. My friends and I were sad, but we all made a decision: we would make our last day our best. We stayed late, just to make it last as long as possible, and pretended that, at least for those few hours, there was no Taliban.

• • • •

My father wanted me to continue to improve my English. So he encouraged me to watch a DVD that one of the journalists had given me: a TV programme called *Ugly Betty*.

I loved Betty, with her big braces and her big heart. I was in awe watching her and her friends as they walked freely down the streets of New York City – with no veils covering their faces and no need for men to accompany them. My favourite part, though, was seeing Betty's father cook for *her* instead of vice versa!

It was odd to watch as Ugly Betty and her friends were free to walk the streets of New York, while we were trapped inside with nothing to do.

All the while, I kept up my blog posts as Gul Makai.

Four days after all girls' schools were shut down, Fazlullah's men destroyed five more schools. *I am quite surprised*, I wrote. *These schools had already been closed. Why did they also need to be destroyed?*

• • • •

During those dark, dull days, we heard rumblings about secret talks with the Taliban. Then, out of nowhere, Fazlullah made a surprising announcement: it was all right for little girls to go to school, he said, but he still insisted that girls over ten should stay home, in purdah.

I was eleven, but I wasn't going to let that stop me. Besides, I could easily pass as a ten-year-old.

Madam Maryam sent out a message to all the girls in the upper school: if they wanted to break the rule, she would open the school doors. The next day, I left home with my books hidden under my shawl and my head held high.

But Mingora had changed while school was closed for the month. The streets were quiet, the stores shuttered, the houses dark. More than one third of the population had run away.

My friends and I were a little bit scared, but we had a plan: if a Talib stopped us, we would just say, "We are in Year Five."

When we arrived at the school gate, Madam Maryam was there, waiting for us. She gave each of us a hug and told us that we were brave. She, too, was taking a big risk being there.

"This secret school," she said, "is our silent protest."

9

• • • •

Displaced

After the *New York Times* documentary aired, we received messages of support from people all over the world. I saw then how powerful the media can be. For the first time, we knew the story of the girls in the Swat Valley was being heard beyond the borders of Pakistan.

But the army and the Taliban were still fighting, and after what was supposed to be a period of peace, the situation got worse. Once again, Mingora was squarely in the middle.

We had stayed through all the other trouble and fighting. But this time, my mother said we should leave and take shelter in Shangla.

• • • •

I stood on our roof, looking at the mountains, at the alleys where we used to play cricket, trying to memorise every detail in case I never saw my home again. Then I went downstairs to start stuffing clothes into a bag. I packed so fast that I took the trousers from one set of shalwar kamiz and the top from another, which meant I ended up with things that didn't match.

I nearly cried when my mother told me I would have to leave my schoolbooks behind. I loved school, and all I cared about were my books!

We were children, after all – children with childish concerns, even with a war on the way.

I hid my books in a bag in our guest room, where it seemed safest, and whispered a few verses of the Holy Quran over them to protect them. Then the whole family gathered together, said some prayers, and put our sweet home in God's protection.

We were about to become internally displaced persons, or **IDPs**. It means you must leave your home because it's too dangerous to stay, but you remain in your own country. Internally displaced persons. That's what we were now, not Pakistanis, not Pashtuns. Our identity had been reduced to three letters: *IDP*.

Outside, the streets were choked with traffic: people and their suitcases, bags of rice, and bedrolls. Entire families balanced on motorbikes – and other people ran down the street with just the clothes on their backs. No one really knew where they were going – just that they had to leave. Two million people were fleeing their homes. It was the biggest exodus in Pashtun history.

The trip, which usually took a few hours, took two days. My father stopped in Peshawar because he felt it was his duty to warn people about what was going on. My mother, brothers and I continued on.

When we finally made it to Shangla, our relatives were shocked to see us. "Why did you come here?" they asked.

The Taliban had only recently left the mountains, but there was a rumour they would be back.

For IDPs, there was no safe place.

Who Is An Internally Displaced Person?

• • • • •

Someone who has been forced to leave his or her home to find safety, but who has not crossed into another country, is called an internally displaced person. More than forty million people in the world today have been displaced because of violence, war, hunger, and many other dangers to their health, safety and human rights.

A refugee is a person who has left his or her home for similar reason, but who has crossed an international border in search of safety. The world now has more than 22.5 million refugees.*

A displaced person who has requested safety in another country and who is awaiting news about whether he or she will be welcomed in is known as an asylum seeker. Close to three million displaced people around the world are seeking asylum right now.

If all these displaced people formed their own country, it would be larger than Great Britain.

---

* Statistics source: UNHCR.

• • • •

I enrolled in school in the village, in the same class as my cousin Sumbul. When we arrived, I saw that only three girls were in Sumbul's year. Most of the girls in Shangla stop going to school after they turn ten, so the few girls who did go were taught alongside the boys.

I stood out in the class: I didn't cover my face the way the other girls did, and I talked freely and asked questions.

Oh, how I missed my home. And my old school. And my books. And even *Ugly Betty*.

In May, the army fought the Taliban for four days in Mingora. From what we heard on the radio, it was impossible to tell who was winning. By the end, there was hand-to-hand combat in the streets.

I tried to picture that: Taliban men fighting in the alley where we played cricket.

The army finally announced that it had

the Taliban on the run, so we breathed a little easier. But we wondered: where would the Taliban go next? Would they return to the mountains?

• • • •

My twelfth birthday took place while we were still waiting to go home. It felt strange. I waited all day for the celebration – but so much had happened that everyone had forgotten. It was hard not to think of how different it had been when I turned eleven. I had shared a cake with my friends. There had been balloons, and I had made a wish for peace in our valley.

I closed my eyes and made that same wish on my twelfth birthday.

10

A Strange Peace

After three months, we were finally on our way home. As we drove down the mountain pass and saw the Swat River, my father began to weep. When we saw the condition of poor Mingora, we were all in tears.

Everywhere we looked, we saw piles of rubble, burned-out cars and smashed windows. Stores had broken front windows and their shelves were empty. It seemed that every building was marked with bullet holes.

The government had said it was safe to go back, but our hometown still felt like a war zone. Army soldiers peered down at us from rooftops, protecting the streets.

The bus station, normally filled with brightly coloured buses and hundreds of travellers, was deserted because most people were still too afraid to return. Weeds were growing up through cracks in the pavement.

But there was no sign of the Taliban.

We had heard that TVs and jewellery had been stolen from the houses surrounding ours. So we held our breath as we saw our overgrown garden and my father unlocked the gate. I ran to the guest room, where I had hidden my books, and discovered that they were safe and sound. I said a prayer of thanks and flicked through them. How lovely to see my quadratic equations, my social studies notes and my English grammar book again.

After everything we had been through, I began to think that becoming a political leader might be a better choice than becoming a doctor. Our country had so many problems. Maybe someday I could help solve them.

• • • •

Swat was finally at peace. The army remained, but the shops reopened, women walked freely in the markets. I planted a mango seed outside our house. I knew it would take a long time for the seed to bear fruit, but it was my way of saying I was full of hope for a long and peaceful future in Mingora.

One of my biggest worries in those days was my height. Around the time I turned thirteen, I stopped growing. Before, I was one of the tallest girls in my class, and now I was among the smallest. I was making a lot of speeches, but I worried that my height made it difficult to get people's attention!

In early 2010 our school was invited to take part in an all-district assembly. Sixty students from all over Swat had been chosen as members. They were mostly boys, but eleven girls from my school participated. And when we held an election for speaker, I won! It was strange to stand on a stage and have people address me as Madam Speaker, but I took the responsibility very seriously.

The assembly met almost every month for a year, and we passed nine resolutions. We decided that no child should be forced to work. We asked for help to send disabled and street children to school. We demanded that all the schools destroyed by the Taliban be rebuilt. Once the resolutions were agreed upon, they were sent to officials – and some were even acted on. We were being heard, we were making a difference, and it felt good.

• • • •

By early 2011 we had heard about more wrecked schools and about how the Taliban were threatening people who'd spoken out against them.

Around the same time, an anonymous letter addressed to my father came to our house. *You have spoken against us, and you will face the consequences.*

It was starting to seem as if the Taliban had never really left.

I tried to tell myself that this terrible letter was an empty threat. But I still prayed for my father's safety every day. I prayed for my school to remain open and for the bombed-out schools to be rebuilt. And I prayed to grow taller. If I was going to become a politician and work for my country, I told God, I would have to at least be able to see over the podium.

11

Good News at Last

One day in October 2011 my father showed me an email I could hardly believe. I had been nominated for an international peace prize. Then I was invited to speak at a conference on education in Lahore, one of Pakistan's largest cities. The chief minister there was starting a network of schools, and to my surprise, he was also giving me an award for my campaign for girls' rights.

I wore my favourite pink shalwar kamiz to

the event and decided that I would tell everyone about how my friends and I had gone against the Taliban's rules and continued going to school secretly. I told the audience: "The girls of Swat were and are not afraid of anyone."

I had been home barely a week when one of my friends ran into class one day and announced that the government had awarded me Pakistan's first National Youth Peace Prize. I couldn't believe it. That day, so many journalists descended on our school. It was a madhouse.

I still hadn't grown an inch by the award ceremony, but I was determined to be heard. When the prime minister presented me with the award, I presented him with a list of demands – including a request that he rebuild the schools Fazlullah destroyed and that the government establish a girls' university in Swat. In that moment, I knew I would become a politician – so I could take action and not just ask for help from others.

When it was announced that the prize would be awarded every year to someone new and be named the Malala Prize in my honour, I noticed a frown on my father's face. In our country's tradition, we don't name things like this after people while they are alive, only after they have died. He was a bit superstitious and thought it a bad omen.

I may have been getting attention from around the world, but I was still the same old Malala to my brothers, who still fought with me and teased me and wrestled with me for the TV remote.

I wondered what my friends thought about all these awards. We were a very competitive group, after all. Would Moniba take up with a new best friend while I was away?

But on my first day back at school, I entered the room and saw all my school friends gathered around a cake, shouting, "Surprise!" They had collected money and bought a white cake with chocolate icing that read SUCCESS FOREVER!

My dear friends only wanted to share in my success. I knew in my heart that any one of us could have achieved what I had; I was lucky I had parents who encouraged me despite the fear we all felt.

"Now you can get back to your schoolwork," Madam Maryam said as we finished our cake.

12

A Threat Against Me

My father and I were meeting with a Pakistani journalist in early 2012 when, with tears in her eyes, she told my father she had something she wanted to show him. They looked at a computer screen with worried faces and then quickly shut it down.

A short while later, my father's phone rang, and he walked away. He came back inside looking very grey. "What is it?"

I asked. "There's something you're not telling me."

My father had always treated me as an equal, but I could see he was trying to decide whether to protect me from this thing or to share it with me. He sighed heavily, then showed me what he'd been looking at on the computer.

He Googled my name. Malala Yousafzai, the Taliban said, "should be killed."

There it was in black-and-white. A death threat against me.

I remembered how nervous I was in 2009, when school first reopened, and I walked to school with my books hidden under my scarf. But I had changed since then. I was three years older now. I had travelled and given speeches and won awards. Here was a call for my death, and I was as calm as could be. It was as if I were reading about someone else.

I took another look at the message on

the screen. Then I closed the computer and never looked at those words again. The worst had happened. I had been targeted by the Taliban. Now I would get back to doing what I was meant to do.

"Are you all right, jani?" asked my dear father, who was near tears.

"***Aba***," I said, trying to reassure him. "Everybody knows they will die someday. No one can stop death. It doesn't matter if it comes from a Talib or from cancer."

But my proud, fearless Pashtun father was shaken in a way I'd never seen. And I knew why. It was one thing for him to be a target of the Taliban. He had always said, "Let them kill me. I will die for what I believe in." But he had never imagined the Taliban would talk about hurting a child. Hurting me.

My father suggested we stop our campaign. I saw the fear in his face, but I also knew he would honour my wishes no matter what I decided. But there was no decision to make. I felt a powerful force inside me, something bigger and stronger than me, and it had made me fearless. Now it was up to me to give my father a dose of the courage he had always given me.

"Aba," I said. "You were the one who said if we believe in something greater than our lives, then our voices will only multiply, even if we are dead. We can't stop now."

He understood. Still, he said we should be careful about what we say and to whom we say it.

As we travelled home, I asked myself what I would do if a Talib came to kill me.

Well, I would just take my shoe and hit him.

But then I reminded myself: *you must not treat others with cruelty. You must fight them with peace and dialogue.*

Malala, I said to myself. *Just tell him what is in your heart. That you want an education. For yourself. For all girls. For his sister, his daughter. For him.*

That's what I would do. Then I would say, "Now you can do what you want."

• • • •

By spring, a tiny miracle in the campaign for education had taken place right in my own home. My mother had started learning to read.

While my father and I were busy speaking across Swat Valley, my mother had started working with one of the teachers at the Khushal primary school. She was soon able to read Pakistan's national language, **Urdu** – and she had started learning English.

My mother loved schoolwork even more than I did, if that was possible. In the evenings, she and I would often do our homework together, sipping tea – two generations of Pashtun women happily huddled over their books.

• • • •

My fifteenth birthday felt like a turning point for me. I was already considered an adult – that happens at age fourteen in our society. But it was time for me to think about my future. I knew for certain now that I wanted to be a political leader. And I started to worry that the awards I was receiving were too much. I saw so many children suffering still – why should I enjoy galas and ceremonies?

I told my father I wanted to spend some of the money I'd received helping people who needed it. I had never forgotten the children I'd seen sorting rubbish at the dump all those years earlier. I wanted to help kids like them. So I organised a meeting with twenty-one girls at school, and we discussed how we could help every girl in Swat get an education. We decided we would focus on street children and those in child labour. We had plans to keep talking, and then in the autumn, we would decide what exactly we could do.

• • • •

In early August my father received some frightening news that Zahid Khan, a close friend of his who also spoke out against the Taliban, had been attacked. We had been told that the Taliban had fled, but there was still violence in the valley. The people most in danger were the ones who were calling for peace.

By some miracle, Zahid Khan survived. After that, though, I noticed a change in my father. Before he stepped inside the school, he looked up and down the street four or five times to be sure he wasn't being followed. At night he would come to my room pretending he was there to say good night. But he was actually checking to make sure all my windows were locked.

"If the Taliban had wanted to kill me," I told him, "they should have done it in 2009. That was their time."

He would shake his head at me and say, "No, you should be safe."

I did worry sometimes that a person could climb over the boundary wall and get into our house. Sometimes, after the rest of the family was asleep, I would tiptoe outside and check the lock on the front gate.

13

A Day Like Any Other

The second Tuesday in October 2012 started out the same as any other. I'd slept in, as usual. I'd stayed up extra late after talking to Moniba, studying for my year-end exam in Pakistani studies.

As I raced out the door that day, I told myself not to worry too much about the exam. I just needed to work hard and thank God for all I had. So I whispered a prayer of thanks. *Oh, and, God*, I added, *please give me first place, since I have worked so hard.*

Our teachers always reminded us, "God won't give you marks if you don't work hard. God showers us with His blessings, but He is honest as well." That is why I always worked hard, too.

• • • •

After the exam, I chatted with Moniba and looked around for my brother Atal, who was supposed to ride home with me that day. But as the rest of the girls gathered around to watch our driver do a magic trick, I forgot all about my mother's instructions about Atal.

We took our usual places in the dyna: Moniba was next to me, and the rest of my friends were across from us on the other bench. A little girl named Hina grabbed the seat next to me, the spot where my friend Shazia usually sat – forcing Shazia to sit on the bench in the middle, where we often put our rucksacks.

Shazia looked so unhappy, I asked Hina to move.

Just as the van was about to pull away, Atal came running. The doors were shut, but he jumped onto the tailboard on the back. This was a dangerous new trick of his, hanging off the tailboard.

"Sit inside, Atal," said the driver.

But Atal didn't budge.

"Sit inside with the girls, Atal Khan Yousafzai, or I won't take you!" the driver said with more force this time.

"I would rather walk than ride home with you!" yelled Atal. He jumped down and stormed off in a huff.

It was hot and sticky inside the dyna as we bounced along Mingora's crowded rush-hour streets, and one of the girls started a song to pass the time. The air was thick with the familiar smell of diesel, bread and kebab mixed with the stench from the nearby stream, where everyone dumped rubbish. We turned off the main road at the army checkpoint as always and passed the poster that read WANTED TERRORISTS.

We passed the Little Giants snack factory, and then the road became oddly quiet. The bus slowed to a halt. I don't remember a young man stopping us and asking the driver if this was the Khushal school bus. I don't remember the other man jumping onto the tailboard and leaning into the back, where we were all sitting. I never heard him ask, "Who is Malala?" And I didn't hear the *crack, crack, crack* of the three bullets.

The last thing I remember is thinking about my exam. After that, everything went black.

PART FOUR

• • • •

A New Life, Far from Home

14

A Place Called Birmingham

I woke up on 16 October to a lot of people standing around looking at me. They all had four eyes, two noses, and two mouths. I blinked, but it did no good. I was seeing everything in double.

The first thing I thought was *Thank God, I'm not dead.*

But I had no idea where I was. The people were speaking English, and since I did, too,

I tried to talk, but no sound came out. A tube of some kind was in my throat. It had stolen my voice.

I was in a high bed, and all around me, complicated machines beeped and purred. I understood then. I was in a hospital.

My heart clenched in panic. Where were my parents? Were they hurt? Something had happened to me, I knew. I was sure something had happened to my father as well.

A nice woman wearing a headscarf came to my side and began to pray in Urdu. Listening to the soothing, beautiful words of the Holy Quran, I closed my eyes and drifted off.

• • • •

When I opened my eyes next, I was in a green room with no windows and very bright lights. A doctor spoke to me in Urdu. His voice was muffled, but I understood enough to hear that I was safe and that he had brought me from Pakistan. I tried to talk but couldn't; a nurse gave me a piece of paper and a pen, but I couldn't write properly. So the nurse wrote the alphabet on a piece of paper, and I pointed at letters.

The first word I spelled out was *father.* Then *country.*

Where was my father? I wanted to know. And what country was this?

The doctor's voice was still hard to hear, but he seemed to be saying that I was in a place called Birmingham. I didn't know where that was. Only later did I figure out it was in England.

Why hadn't he said anything about my father? I moved to spell out *father* again, and a pain cut through my head. It was as if a hundred razors were inside my skull, clattering and rattling around. I tried to breathe. The nurse dabbed at my left ear, and blood came away on the cloth. Why was my ear bleeding? What had happened to me?

Nurses and doctors came in and out,

asking me questions. I nodded and shook my head in reply. They asked if I knew my name. I nodded. They asked if I could move my left hand. I shook my head. They had so many questions, and yet they wouldn't answer mine.

• • • •

A lady walked in and told me her name was Dr. Fiona Reynolds. She spoke to me as if we were old friends. She handed me a green teddy bear – which I thought was an odd colour for it – and a pink notebook. The first thing I wrote was *Thank you*.

Then I wrote, *Why I have no father?*

And, as I looked around the room at all the complicated medical equipment, I wrote, *My father has no money. Who will pay for this?*

"Your father is safe," she said. "He is in Pakistan. Don't worry about the payment."

If my father was safe, why wasn't he here? And where was my mother?

The words I needed would not come to my mind. She seemed to understand. "Something bad happened to you," she said. "But you're safe now."

What had happened? I tried to remember. During those first days of being in the hospital, I drifted in and out of a dreamworld. All sorts of images floated through my head.

I see a crowd gathered around me as I lie on a bed, or maybe a stretcher. I can't see my father, and I'm trying to cry out, *Where is Aba, where is my father?* But I can't speak. And then I see him, and I feel joy and relief.

I am on a stretcher, and my father is reaching out to me.

I am trying to wake up, to go to school, but I can't. Then I see my school and my friends, and I can't reach them.

These images seemed very real, yet I knew they couldn't all be. But somehow I had ended up in this place called Birmingham, in a room full of machines, with only the green teddy bear at my side.

I thought I had been shot, but I wasn't sure – were those dreams or memories?

I couldn't remember words, either. I wrote to the nurses asking for a *wire to clean my teeth.*

Then I saw that my green teddy bear was gone. A white one had taken its place. But the green teddy had been by my side; he had helped me. I took the notebook and wrote, *Where's the green teddy?*

No one gave me the answer I wanted. They told me it was the same teddy that Dr. Fiona had given me. The lights and walls had given him a green glow, but the teddy was white, they said. He was always white.

The bright lights in my room were like hot daggers to my eyes. *Stop lights*, I begged in my notebook.

The nurses did their best to darken the room, but as soon as I got some relief from the pain, my mind kept spinning back to the same question: Where was my father?

Every time a different doctor or nurse came into my room, I handed them the notebook and pointed to the questions about my father. They all said not to worry.

But I did worry. I couldn't stop.

I thought for sure that the doctors and nurses were all saying, "Malala doesn't have any money. Malala can't pay for her treatment." One doctor always looked sad, so I wrote him a note. *Why are you sad?* I asked. I thought it was because he knew I couldn't pay. But he replied, "I'm not sad."

Who will pay? I wrote. *We don't have any money.*

"Don't worry," he said. After that, he always smiled when he saw me.

• • • •

Dr. Fiona came into my room and handed me a newspaper clipping. It was a picture of my father standing next to the Pakistan army's chief of staff. My father was alive! And in the background of the photo was Atal!

I smiled, feeling thankful. Then I noticed a figure in a shawl sitting in the back of the photo near my brother. I could just make out her feet. Those were my mother's feet!

That's my mother! I wrote to Dr. Fiona.

I slept a bit better that night, though it was still a sleep full of strange dreams. I would wake up and look around for the green teddy. But always it was just the white one.

Now that I knew my family was safe, I spent all my time worrying about how we would pay for my treatment. Was my father at home, selling our few possessions? Was he calling on his friends to ask for a loan?

When the man who had spoken to me in Urdu, Dr. Javid Kayani, came in with his mobile phone and said, "We're going to call your parents," I couldn't believe it.

"You won't cry," he said firmly but kindly.

"You will be strong. We don't want your family to worry."

I nodded. I hadn't cried once since I'd arrived. My left eye was constantly weeping, but I had not cried.

After a series of blips and beeps, I heard my father's dear and familiar voice. "Jani?" he said. "How are you feeling, my jani?"

I couldn't reply because of the tube in my throat. And I couldn't smile because my face was numb. But I was smiling inside, and I knew my father knew that.

"I'll come soon," my father said. "Now have a rest, and in two days we will be there."

His voice was loud and bright. Maybe a little too bright.

Then I realised: he had also been told not to cry.

15

A Hundred Questions

I wrote a new note in my pink diary. *Mirror.*

When I got my wish, I was surprised by what I saw. Half of my head was shaved, and my long hair was gone. Stitches dotted my left brow. A huge purple-and-yellow bruise surrounded my left eye. My face was swollen to the size of a melon. And the left corner of my mouth turned down in a frown.

Who was this poor, strange-looking Malala? And what had happened to her?

Now my hair is small was all I could write.

Had the Taliban shaved my head? I wondered.

Who did this to me? I wrote, my letters scrambled. *What happened to me?*

Dr. Fiona said what she always said. "Something bad happened to you, but you are safe."

But this time it wasn't enough. *Was I shot?* I wrote. I couldn't move the pencil fast enough to keep up with my questions. Had anyone else been hurt? I wondered. Had there been a bomb?

Frustrated, I started to squirm. I saw the mobile phone on Dr. Fiona's belt and signalled to her that I wanted it – I mimed dialing on my palm, then brought the "phone" to my ear.

Dr. Fiona placed a gentle hand on my wrist. She began to speak slowly and calmly. "You were shot," she said. "On the bus, on your way home from school."

So they did it, I thought. The Taliban really did what they said they would do. I was furious. Not that they'd shot me. That I hadn't had a chance to talk to them. Now they'd never hear what I had to say.

"Two other girls were hurt," Dr. Fiona said. "But they're all right. Shazia and Kainat."

I didn't recognise these names. Or if I did, I couldn't remember who these girls were.

She explained that the bullet had grazed my temple, near my left eye, and travelled eighteen inches down to my left shoulder, where it stopped. It could have taken out my eye or gone into my brain, she said. "It's a miracle you're alive."

I tried to speak but remembered I couldn't. So I looked back in the mirror.

I will admit that I used to be sensitive about my looks. I had thought that my nose was too big. My skin was too dark. Even my toes were too long.

But I looked at this Malala in the mirror with nothing but curiosity. I was like a scientist studying a specimen. I wanted to understand exactly where the bullet went, what exactly it had done.

I wasn't saddened by what I saw. I wasn't scared. I just thought: *it doesn't matter what I look like. I am alive.*

I saw that Dr. Fiona had put a box of tissues between us and realised that she'd been expecting me to cry. Maybe the old Malala would have cried. But now the funny face in the mirror was simply proof that I was still here on this Earth.

I wanted to learn more. Had the bullet passed through my brain? Was that why I couldn't hear properly? Why couldn't I shut my left eye?

I had a hundred questions for Dr. Fiona, but I asked only one. *How soon can I go home?*

• • • •

I stared at the clock in my room while I waited for my family. Watching the hands move around the dial reassured me that I was, indeed, alive. It also helped me measure off the minutes until my family arrived.

The clock had always been my enemy at home – stealing my sleep in the morning when all I wanted to do was hide under the blanket. Wait until my family heard that I had finally made friends with the clock – and that, for the first time in my life, I was waking up early! Every morning, I waited eagerly for seven AM, when friends like Yma, who worked at the hospital, and nurses from the children's hospital would come and help me pass the hours.

When I could see well enough, they brought me a DVD player and a stack of DVDs.

They had turned on the TV during my first days, but my vision was still so blurry that I had asked them to turn it off. Now my eyesight was better, although I was still seeing double a bit. So I got to choose from *Bend It Like Beckham*, *High School Musical*, *Hannah Montana*, and *Shrek*. I chose *Shrek*. I loved it so much I watched the sequel right after.

One of the nurses figured out that if she covered my damaged eye with a cotton patch, my double vision wasn't as bad. So I passed the day with a green ogre and a talking donkey and waited for my parents to come to England.

• • • •

After a few days in the hospital, the tube in my throat was removed, and I got my voice back. So I began asking Dr. Fiona my questions. It was like being back in biology class at school.

I learned that back in Pakistan, the doctors told my parents that I wouldn't survive unless I was moved to a better hospital. My parents agreed to let me go with Dr. Javid and

Dr. Fiona. The two doctors, who happened to have been in Pakistan for other work and were brought in to help treat me, had been by my side for nearly two weeks. No wonder they behaved as if they'd known me for ever.

I wanted to know one last thing: "I was in a coma," I said. "For how long?"

"A week," Dr. Fiona told me.

I had missed a week of my life. And in that time, I'd been shot, I had an operation, and I had been flown to the other side of the world. The first time I had ever flown out of Pakistan was on a private jet to save my life.

The world had gone on all around me, and I knew nothing about it. I wondered what else I had missed out on.

16

• • • •

Filling in the Blanks

My father had told me on the phone that he would be by my side in two days. But two days turned into two more. Dr. Javid arranged another call to Pakistan. My father promised that the whole family would be there soon – just one more day.

I didn't believe they were actually coming until Dr. Javid tilted up my bed so I would be sitting to greet them. By then, it had been sixteen days since I had run out of my house in Mingora. I had been in four hospitals and travelled thousands of miles.

During this time, I had not cried once. Not when the nurses removed the staples in my head, not when their needles pricked my skin, not when the light was like a dagger in my eyes. But when the door opened, and I heard familiar voices saying *jani* and *pisho*, and when everyone fell upon me, weeping and kissing my hands because they were afraid to touch me, finally, I cried. I cried and cried and cried some more. Oh, how I cried.

For the first time in my life, I was even happy to see those annoying little brothers of mine. After sixteen of the most frightening days of our lives, we were all together again.

My parents tried to hide their concern about me, but I could see it in their eyes. Who could blame them? I knew from looking in the mirror that half my face was not working, and half my hair was gone. As soon as I spoke with Atal and saw his surprised face, I realised how strange I sounded: I was still speaking only in simple, baby sentences, as if I were three years old.

Don't worry, I wanted to say. *The old Malala is still in here.*

I smiled to try to reassure them, but a shadow darkened my mother's face. I thought I was grinning – but my parents saw something that looked like an awkward, crooked frown.

• • • •

"Everything is fine. We are all here now," my father would say when I asked about what had happened to me. Then he would try to change the subject, and I would let him.

But one day, when we were alone, he grasped my hand, his eyes filled with tears. "Jani, they threatened me many times. You have taken my bullet. It should have been me." And then he said, "People experience both joy and suffering in their lives. Now you have had all the suffering at once, and the rest of your life will be filled with only joy." He could not go on.

I longed to tell him that I wasn't suffering – and that I didn't want him to suffer, either. I smiled my crooked smile and said simply, "Aba." It was so unfair that my poor injured brain couldn't come up with the words for the person I loved so much.

But my father understood. He smiled back through teary eyes.

A little while later my mother was helping me in the bathroom when I saw her sneak a look at my reflection in the mirror. Our eyes met for a moment, then she looked away.

Then came a whisper. "Your face," she said. "Will it get better?"

I told her what the doctors had told me: my face would eventually improve. But it would never be quite the same as before.

When she walked me back to my bed, I looked at my parents. "It's my face," I said.

"And I accept it. Now," I said gently, "you must accept it, too."

There was so much more I wanted to say to my parents. I'd had time to get used to my new face. But it was a shock to them. *When you see death*, I wanted to say, *things change*. It didn't matter if I couldn't blink or smile. I was still me, Malala.

I knew my recovery was a blessing, a gift from God and from all the people who had cared for me and prayed for me. So I was at peace. But while I was in Birmingham healing, watching Shrek and his talking donkey, my poor parents had been thousands of miles away, suffering their own terrible pain.

From that day on, our family began to heal together.

• • • •

My parents slowly filled me in on what had happened in the sixteen days between the shooting and our reunion.

What I learned was this:

As soon as the bus driver, Usman Bhai Jan, realised what had happened, he drove me straight to Swat Central Hospital. The other girls were screaming and crying. I was lying on Moniba's lap, bleeding.

That day, my father was at a meeting of the Association of Private Schools, where he was giving a speech. When he learned what had happened, he rushed off to the hospital. He found me inside, lying on a stretcher, a bandage over my head, my eyes closed, my hair spread out.

"My daughter, you are my brave daughter, my beautiful daughter," he said to me over and over, as if saying it could awaken me. I think that, somehow, I did know he was there, even though I was not conscious.

The doctors told my father that the bullet had not gone near my brain and that the injury wasn't serious. Soon, the army took charge, and by three p.m., I was in an ambulance on the way to a helicopter that would take me to another hospital, in the city of Peshawar. There was no time to wait for my mother, so Madam Maryam, who had arrived at the hospital soon after my father, insisted on coming in case I needed a woman's help.

"Don't cry," my mother had said to our tearful neighbours. "Pray." As the helicopter flew over our street, she rushed up to the roof. She took her scarf off her head, a rare gesture for a Pashtun woman, and lifted it up to the sky. "God, I entrust her to you," she said.

Pakistani TV channels showed pictures and videos of me, with prayers and poems. Poor Atal turned on the TV after school, heard the news, and realised that if he hadn't had a tantrum about riding on the tailboard, he would have been on that bus, too.

Meanwhile, I was in Peshawar, where a doctor had discovered that my injuries were quite serious. He operated on me, and then the two British doctors – Dr. Fiona and

Dr. Javid– took over my care.

Dr. Fiona insisted that I would receive the best care at Dr. Javid's own hospital in Birmingham, England: Queen Elizabeth Hospital. But I needed to be moved immediately – within two days. My family couldn't go with me. Dr. Javid assured my father that I would be taken care of.

"Isn't it a miracle you all happened to be here when Malala was shot?" my father said.

"It is my belief God sends the solution first and the problem later," replied Dr. Javid.

• • • •

I had missed so much! And yet, as my parents told me everything that had happened and that the whole world knew about it, it was almost as if they were telling me a story. That these things had happened to some other girl, not me.

Perhaps that's because I do not remember a thing about the shooting. Not one single thing.

The doctors and nurses had complicated

explanations for that: the brain protects us from memories that are too painful to remember. Or, they said, my brain might have shut down as soon as I was injured. I love science, but I don't need it to know why I don't remember the attack.

I know why: God is kind to me.

People don't understand when I say this. I suppose unless you have been close to death, you cannot understand. But death and I have been very close. And death, it seems, did not want me.

• • • •

When I finally watched the news, I learned that a spokesman for Fazlullah said the Taliban had been "forced" to shoot me because I would not stop speaking out against them.

They had warned me, they told the press, but I wouldn't stop.

My other crimes? I spoke for education and peace. In their terms, I was speaking for Western education, which was against

Islam, in their opinion.

The Taliban would try again to kill me, Fazlullah said. "Let this be a lesson."

It was a lesson, indeed. My mother was right when she quoted from the Holy Quran. "Falsehood has to die," she had told me all those years earlier, when I was considering doing the blog for the BBC. "And truth has to come forward."

Truth will always triumph over lies. This is the true Islamic belief that has guided us on our journey.

The Taliban shot me to try to silence me. But the whole world was listening to my message now.

17

• • • •

Messages from Around the World

One day I received a bag of cards. It was around the time of Eid ul-Azha, "Big Eid," one of the holiest of Muslim holidays. So I thought, *How nice, friends have sent me cards for Eid.* But how did they know where I was? I wondered.

Then I noticed the postage dates. 16 October, 17 October. These were the days soon after the shooting. These cards had nothing to do with Eid. They were from people all over the

world wishing me a speedy recovery. Many were from children. I was astonished at how many cards there were.

I learned that there were eight thousand cards and letters for me. Some were addressed simply "Malala, Birmingham Hospital." One was addressed "Girl Shot in the Head, Birmingham."

There were parcels, too. Boxes of chocolate. And teddy bears of every size. Most precious of all, perhaps, was a parcel sent by the children of Benazir Bhutto. Inside were two scarves that had belonged to their mother, who was the first female prime minister in the Islamic world – and one of my biggest role models.

Apparently, many people had tried to visit me. Journalists, celebrities, and a number of politicians. But the hospital had kept them away so I could heal in private.

But now I saw that famous actors and singers had tweeted about me and had wished me well on Facebook. It was exciting, overwhelming, and – because my brain was still not working right – confusing.

How did these celebrities even know who I was?

While I was in a windowless room, unaware of what was happening in the outside world, the outside world knew exactly what had happened to me. I learned that more than two hundred journalists from around the world had come to the hospital to see me. Except for that one day when I tried to watch the BBC, I hadn't seen the news since I had arrived. But now I understood: I *was* the news.

How amazing. While I was feeling so alone in this hospital, wondering about my family, worrying about how we would pay for my care, people from all around the world were worrying about *me*! I didn't feel so lonely anymore.

I couldn't wait to get home and tell Moniba about the celebrities!

• • • •

In December, after nearly two months inside hospitals, I was finally permitted my first trip outside: to the Birmingham Botanical Gardens. My mother and I went with two nurses. My father didn't go; he had become so recognisable from TV he was afraid he would attract cameras.

On the way, I sat in the backseat of the car,

turning my head from side to side, overjoyed to take in everything in a country that was brand-new to me.

I wasn't used to the harsh wind and crisp, cold air. But the plants! They were gorgeous. And familiar! "This one is in my valley, too," I told one of the nurses. "This one, too!"

My mother was so excited she called my father. "For the first time," she said, "I am happy."

By this time, my family was living in an apartment in a tall tower in Birmingham and visiting me every day. And in a sure sign that life was getting back to normal, my brothers were driving me crazy! After about a day of treating me like a china doll, they were back to being annoying "What is all this fuss over Malala?" said Atal. "I have seen her. She survived."

"Leave those two at home!" I begged my parents. "They do nothing but make noise and try to take the gifts I've received."

I was finally able to read again, and my language and memory started to come back, too. Though I still had a hard time remembering some of my friends' names, I was making steady improvements, and my spirits got better every day.

Also that month, I had my first visitor from outside the family – Asif Ali Zardari, the president of Pakistan.

The hospital was afraid that the visit would attract too much attention from reporters, but it was an essential one. Mr. Zardari had pledged that the government would cover all my medical costs.

I was bundled up in a purple parka and sneaked out of the building through the staff exit. We drove right past a flock of journalists and photographers, and they didn't even notice. It was like something out of a spy novel.

We were driven to some kind of office, and while we waited, Atal, Khushal and I played a computer game called Elf Bowling. This was my first time playing it, and I still beat both of them. More proof that the old Malala was back.

When the president came in, he laid a hand on my head, a gesture of respect in my country. He told us he had arranged for my father to have a job in Birmingham. Everything would be fine, he said. My job was to concentrate on my recovery.

Afterward, Mr. Zardari said I was "a remarkable girl and a credit to Pakistan."

It was an amazing day. The leader of my country was treating me with respect, and all my worries about money were lifted.

But, oh, it was a bittersweet day, too. Because I understood: we would not be going home for a long time.

18

• • • •

Miracles

Finally, I was released from the hospital, and 2013 was off to a happy start. It was so good to be home with my family, even though this home was an apartment in a tall building with a lift. I would have given anything to really be home, but what mattered most was that my family was finally together again.

I tried to build up strength by walking in the brisk air. But I still couldn't hear properly, so I was constantly turning this way and that to see what was going on. A simple trip to the grocery store could be overwhelming. Overwhelming – and fascinating.

In Birmingham's cafés, we saw men and women talking together in a way that would be unimaginable in Swat. And the women wore tiny shorts, bare legs, and high heels, even in winter. "Are their legs made of iron, so they don't feel the cold?" asked my mother.

• • • •

I missed home terribly. I missed my school friends, I missed the mountains, the waterfall, the beautiful Swat River, and the lush green fields. So it came as hard news when I found out that some people in Pakistan were critical of me. People who questioned our family's honesty. People who even said my father had shot me as a stunt so we could live overseas in luxury.

The other news was from school: over Skype, Moniba told me that she missed me and how no other girl could take my place in her heart.

She also told me that Shazia and Kainat were recovered and back in school. And she told me my friends were still saving a seat for me in class.

"Oh, by the way," she said. "You scored a one hundred percent on your Pakistani studies exam." That was the test I'd taken the morning of the shooting.

• • • •

I had many surgeries, including one to improve my hearing. A tiny electronic hearing aid was placed behind my ear. A few weeks after that, I was fitted with a receiver, and then I heard a tiny beep. Then another. Then came the sound of the doctor's voice. At first, everyone sounded like a robot, but soon my hearing got better.

How great God is! He has given us eyes to see the beauty of the world, hands to touch it, a nose to experience all its fragrance, and a heart to appreciate it all. But we don't realise how miraculous our senses are until we lose one.

The return of my hearing was just one miracle.

A Talib had fired three shots at point-blank range at three girls in a school bus – and none of us were killed.

One person had tried to silence me. And millions spoke out.

Those were miracles, too.

19

This New Place

We have settled now into our Birmingham life, in a tidy brick house on a tree-lined street. It is lovely. Calm. And too quiet. No children play cricket in the alleys. No women sit on the back porch and have a good gossip.

But when we go for a walk in the main shopping district in Birmingham, I am amazed by the different kinds of people: freckle-faced boys in football tops, men in business suits and women in business suits, conservative Muslim women in burqas and young Muslim women in jeans and headscarves.

Sometimes people ask to take a picture with me. I don't mind. I understand that these are the same people who gave me support when I needed it and who give me courage now to keep going. It's odd to be so well known but to be lonely at the same time.

• • • •

At my new school, I wear a British schoolgirl's uniform: a green jumper, striped button-down shirt, tights and a blue skirt. A handful of Muslim girls in my class wear their skirts down to their ankles, as I do. Other girls roll their skirts up even shorter as soon as they arrive at school. I think: *what an interesting country this is, where some girls are free to cover their bodies and others are free not to.*

Here we also have projectors and laptops, videos and Wi-Fi, and classes such as music, art and computer science, and even cooking (which I dislike). Sometimes I wish I were back home in Pakistan, where school was just a teacher and a chalkboard. Other times I feel sad that my old friends don't have all this fancy technology and these special classes. But then I remember that they have what I don't: one another.

My new schoolmates and I don't always get one another's jokes, and I cannot be as free, or as cheeky, as they can. I am a good girl – I always have been. But now, I tell myself, I must take extra care with what I say and do. A lot of people are counting on me.

In Pakistan, I was just Malala. Here, at least at the beginning, I was "Malala, the girl who was shot by the Taliban." I wanted to just be Malala again, a normal girl.

Yes, I have seen and experienced things that my new friends couldn't even imagine. But as time went on, I realised they have had experiences *I* can't imagine. What I'm finding is that we have much more in common than we have different, and every day we learn something new from one another. Every day I feel a little bit more like plain old Malala, just another girl in the class.

• • • •

Until we can go home to Pakistan, we can bring it to us, when friends and family come to visit. My mother is happiest with extra chairs around the dinner table. As her happiness grows, so does her willingness to try new things. She has begun to learn English again. She has even allowed herself to be photographed.

My father may not be a school headmaster anymore, but he still goes to conferences on girls' education and speaks out for peace. At first, it was strange to him that people wanted to hear from him because of me, and not the other way around. "Malala used to be known as my daughter," he says. "But I am proud to say that now I am known as Malala's father."

My father, meanwhile, has taken on a new responsibility at home. I teased him that while he and I are busy speaking about women's rights, my mother is still doing the cooking and cleaning. Now he cooks every morning. It's the same thing every time: fried eggs. His cooking may not be full of flavour, but it is full of love.

• • • •

As the first anniversary of the shooting approached, and journalists began to interview me, I discovered that I was not nearly as upset as some of them were about what had happened to me. I guess I see my situation differently. If you tell yourself, "Malala, you can never go home because you are the target of the Taliban," you just keep suffering.

I look at it this way: I can see! I can hear! I can talk! I am living the life God wants for me.

The journalists also ask if I am afraid. I say no. And that is true.

I am frustrated when journalists want to focus on the attack, rather than on my fight for girls' education. I understand it. But in my mind, out of the violence and tragedy came opportunity.

I never forget that opportunity, especially when I think about the organisation that I started to help other kids, Malala Fund, and remember all the good it has done and will

What Is Malala Fund?

• • • • •

As I was recovering from my attack, my father and I knew that we needed to find a way to continue our fight to help girls in need get a free, safe and high-quality education. Girls just like me. That was the beginning of Malala Fund.

As people reached out wanting to help us, we gathered their generous donations and put them toward our cause. Our first gift was to help forty girls in my home, Pakistan's Swat Valley. Through Malala Fund, we were able to give them money for uniforms, shoes, materials, and much more. When we gave that gift, we set a goal that we would someday reach forty million girls.

We are now on our way. What began with just two people speaking out for what we believed was right has become a worldwide effort involving thousands and thousands of girls. We have opened schools – including one in Lebanon for Syrian refugee girls – met with dozens of prime ministers and presidents, and, most important, connected with thousands of girls, so that we could share their stories with the world.

do. We are helping girls in Swat who have no education because they were forced to work. We are helping refugee children all over the world. It's our duty to help these children get food, shelter, and an education. And we will.

I think of the world as a family. When one of us is suffering, we must all pitch in and help. Because when people say they support me, they are really saying they support girls' education.

So, yes, the Taliban shot me. But they can only shoot a body. They cannot kill my beliefs, and they cannot stop my campaign to see every child in school. I am still here for a reason, and it is to use my life to help people.

20

• • • •

One Girl Among Many

For my sixteenth birthday, I was given the most extraordinary gift: I was invited to speak at the United Nations in New York City. On that day, 12 July 2013, which the UN had named Malala Day, four hundred people would be in attendance: high-ranking officials from all over the world, as well as ordinary children like me. It would be so different from the fearful birthdays I had spent in Pakistan not long ago.

My whole family travelled to New York. We saw *Annie* on Broadway, and we stayed in a hotel where they bring pizza to your room on a silver tray. I liked the hustle and bustle of New York, compared with sleepy Birmingham. And I felt as if the city were my old friend after seeing it on *Ugly Betty*. I couldn't wait to tell Moniba: America is a very nice place, but New York was just as loud and crowded as other cities I've seen, with its honking horns and people rushing here and there.

It didn't seem possible that I was going to address the United Nations. I dressed slowly that morning, putting on my favourite pink shalwar kamiz and one of Benazir Bhutto's scarves. Then I stood up and spoke not just to the audience but to every person around the world who could take courage from my words:

Dear brothers and sisters,
Do remember one thing. Malala Day
is not my day. Today is the day of every

woman, every boy, and every girl who has raised their voice for their rights. Thousands of people have been killed by the terrorists, and millions have been injured. I am just one of them.

So here I stand... one girl among many.

I speak not for myself, but for all girls and boys.

I raise up my voice not so that I can shout, but so that those without a voice can be heard.

Those who have fought for their rights:

Their right to live in peace.

Their right to be treated with dignity.

Their right to equality of opportunity.

Their right to be educated.

On the ninth of October 2012, the Taliban shot me on the left side of my forehead. They shot my friends, too. They thought that the bullets would silence us. But they failed. And then, out of that silence came thousands of voices. The terrorists thought that they would change our aims and stop our ambitions, but nothing changed in my life except this: weakness, fear, and hopelessness died. Strength, power, and courage was born. I am the same Malala. My ambitions are the same. My hopes are the same. My dreams are the same.

One child, one teacher, one book and one pen can change the world.

As I heard the applause and took my seat, all I could think of was that I had come a long way from being Malala the toddler, giving lessons to the empty chairs at the Khushal School. Or Malala the girl who gave speeches to the bathroom mirror. Somehow, by the grace of God, I really was speaking to millions of people.

I had once asked God to make me taller.

I have realised that God has answered my prayer, making me as tall as the sky, with a voice that can reach people everywhere. With my height, I have been given a responsibility and a gift: the responsibility to make the world a more peaceful place, which I carry with me every moment of every day; and the gift to be able to do so.

Peace in every home, every street, every village, every country – this is my dream. Education for every boy and every girl in the world.

I am Malala. My world has changed, but I have not.

Epilogue

• • • •

The Youngest Person Ever

In October 2014, almost two years to the day after I was attacked, I received a great honour. I became the youngest person ever to be awarded the Nobel Peace Prize. I was in chemistry class when I found out. The deputy head teacher came and called me outside. Was I in trouble? I thought.

When she told me I had won the Nobel Peace Prize alongside children's rights activist Kailash Satyarthi, I was shocked. I responded

What Is the Nobel Peace Prize?

• • • • •

Named for scientist Alfred Nobel, the first Nobel Peace Prize was awarded in 1901. Winners are chosen by a committee of five people in Norway, but anyone is eligible – no matter who they are or where they are from – as long as they worked to promote peace for "the greatest benefit to mankind." Past winners include Martin Luther King Jr., Barack Obama, and Doctors without Borders.

Kailash Satyarthi and I received it in 2014 for our "struggle against the suppression of children and young people and for the right of all children to education."

The more I learned about Kailash, the more precious it felt to share the award with him. He works tirelessly to rescue children from slavery and child labour. This kind and committed man leads by example, showing that adults have the responsibility to protect children. He shows that love and kindness can make a difference.

I am so grateful that the Nobel Peace Prize was awarded to recognise the rights of children.

very formally. I thanked her for the news and said I was honoured. It was only when I saw tears in my teachers' eyes when they congratulated me that the meaning of the news really sank in. Everyone was happy for me, and I was happy, too, because the cause that had been a part of my life for so long had been recognised in such an important way.

The ceremony itself was beautiful and inspiring. I was happy to be joined by my brave friends from Pakistan, Shazia and Kainat, as well as girls I've met while travelling with Malala Fund. They have also had to stand up for their rights. It meant so much to me that we could experience the Nobel ceremony together.

I have worked tirelessly in my role as an education activist through Malala Fund. We are growing our work every day, but I know there is so much left to do. I thank God that I have been given this platform. This is my life's work, my mission, and my dream.

• • • •

So much has changed these past few years. Now I live in Oxford, England, where I attend the university. But I am the same old Malala who was going to school in Swat. My life has changed, but I have not. If you were to ask my mother, she would say, "Well, maybe Malala has become wiser, but she's still the same messy girl at home whose shirt is in one place, trousers in another, and who's always crying, 'I haven't done my homework!' "

Some things, even if they are small, do stay the same.

Many of our friends in Pakistan might think we are lucky to live in England, but when you are exiled from your homeland, where your father and forefathers were born and where you have centuries of history, it's very sad. You can no longer touch the soil or hear the sweet sound of the rivers. Fancy hotels and meetings in palaces cannot replace the sense of your true home.

People's love and encouragement give me the energy to continue my fight. I will never give up advocating for peace and education for all. I want to build schools and make sure qualified teachers are in as many places as I can. That is something else that hasn't changed: I am the same stubborn girl who will never give up.

GLOSSARY

aba: affectionate Pashto term, "father"

Allah: the Arabic word for "God"

al-Qaeda: a militant Islamist organisation

badal: revenge

burqa: a garment or robe worn by some Muslim women to cover their bodies in public

dyna: open-backed van or truck

fedayeen: devotees of Islam

haram: prohibited in Islam

Holy Quran: the Muslim holy book

IDP: internally displaced person

imam: local preacher

jani: dear one

madrasa: school for Islamic instruction

mufti: Islamic scholar

mullah: an informal name for an imam or a religious leader

Pashto: the native language of Pashtuns

pisho: cat, kitten

purdah: (of women) segregation or seclusion, wearing the veil

Ramadan: time of inner reflection during the ninth month of the Islamic calendar; observed by fasting every day from sunrise to sunset

shalwar kamiz: traditional outfit of loose tunic (*kamiz*) and trousers (*shalwar*)

Talib: historically, a religious student, but has come to mean a member of the Taliban militant group

Taliban: an Islamic fundamentalist movement

Urdu: the national language of Pakistan

PRONUNCIATION GUIDE

• • • •

burqa: *BURR-ka*

Eid: *EED*

haram: *ha-RAHM*

madrasa: *mah-DRAH-suh*

Malala Yousafzai: *Ma-LA-la YOO-sef-zigh*

(Holy) Quran: *ke-RAN*

A TIME LINE OF MALALA'S LIFE

• • • •

12 July 1997: Malala is born in the Swat Valley in Mingora, Pakistan.

September 2008: As the Taliban threatens to close schools, Malala speaks out about the importance of education.

3 January 2009: Malala begins writing for the BBC Urdu website about life under the Taliban.

15 January 2009: The Taliban's closure of girls' schools goes into effect.

May 2009: Due to unrest, Malala's family and all residents of Swat must leave.

October 2009: The *New York Times* features Malala and her father in a documentary film called *Class Dismissed.*

2009–2010: Malala appears on television speaking for girls' education rights.

October 2011: Desmond Tutu nominates Malala for the International Children's Peace Prize.

December 2011: Malala wins Pakistan's first National Youth Peace Prize.

9 October 2012: Malala is shot by the Taliban on her way home from school.

15 October 2012: Malala is transported to Birmingham, England, for further treatment.

March 2013: Malala returns to school in Birmingham.

12 July 2013: Malala addresses the United Nations on her sixteenth birthday, which is declared Malala Day.

October 2013: Malala and her father set up Malala Fund.

July 2014: Malala travels to Nigeria to speak out against the mass kidnapping of girls.

December 2014: Malala becomes the youngest Nobel Peace Prize recipient in history. In December, she travels to Sweden to accept the award, which she shares with children's rights activist Kailash Satyarthi.

12 July 2015: Malala opens a school in Bekaa Valley, Lebanon, for Syrian refugee girls.

October 2015: The documentary *He Named Me Malala* is released internationally.

September 2016: Malala launches a #YesAllGirls campaign supporting girls' education.

April–September 2017: Malala travels the world on her Girl Power Trip, speaking directly to girls and world leaders alike.

October 2017: Malala attends the University of Oxford.

ABOUT THE AUTHORS

• • • •

MALALA YOUSAFZAI started her campaign for girls' education at the age of ten, when the Swat Valley was being attacked by terrorists, and education was threatened. Using the pen name Gul Makai, she wrote about life under the Taliban for BBC Urdu. Malala also volunteered to be featured in a *New York Times* documentary about education in Pakistan. She used every opportunity to speak publicly for peace and every child's right to an education.

In October 2012 Malala was targeted by the Taliban and shot while returning home from school. She survived and continues her campaign for education.

In 2011, in recognition of her courage and advocacy, Malala was nominated for the International Children's Peace Prize and won Pakistan's first National Youth Peace Prize. She is the youngest person ever to be awarded a Nobel Peace Prize and has received numerous other awards, including the International Children's Peace Prize (2013), the Sakharov Prize for Freedom of Thought, and the Amnesty International Ambassador of Conscience Award.

Malala now attends University of Oxford in England and continues to champion universal access to education through Malala Fund (malala.org), a nonprofit organisation that invests in community-led programs and supports education advocates around the world.

PATRICIA McCORMICK is a two-time National Book Award finalist and author of several critically acclaimed novels for young adults, including *Cut*, *Sold* and *Never Fall Down*. For more information, go to patriciamccormick.com.